HEALTH MATTERS

UNDERSTANDING ANXIETY

BY
HOLLY DUHIG

PowerKiDS press

New York

Published in 2019 by The Rosen Publishing Group
29 East 21st Street, New York, NY 10010

Copyright © 2018 Booklife Publishing
This edition is published by arrangement with Booklife Publishing

Edited by: Kristy Holmes
Designed by: Drue Rintoul

Image Credits
All images are courtesy of Shutterstock.com, unless otherwise specified. With thanks to Getty Images, Thinkstock Photo and iStockphoto.
Front Cover – Africa Studio. 2 – pixelheadphoto digitalskillet. 4&5 – Studio 1One, Carla Francesca Castagno. 6&7 – mike mols, Alohaflaminggo. 8&9 – Designua. 10&11 – CLIPAREA | Custom media, daseugen. 12&13 – TinnaPong, shurkin_son. 14&15 – Antonio Guillem, Alfa Photostudio. 16&17 – michaeljung, Photographee. eu. 18&19 – fredredhat, wavebreakmedia. 20&21 – Monkey Business Images, Jevanto Productions. 22&23 – tanaphongpict, Zurijeta, sirtravelalot. 24&25 – Wasitt Hemwarapornchai, India Picture, pixelheadphoto digitalskillet. 26&27 – Olimpik. 28&29 – SergiyN, Image Point Fr. 30 – Andrey_Popov.

Cataloging-in-Publication Data

Names: Duhig, Holly.
Title: Understanding anxiety / Holly Duhig.
Description: New York : PowerKids Press, 2019. | Series: Health matters | Includes glossary and index.
Identifiers: LCCN ISBN 9781538338421 (pbk.) | ISBN 9781538338414 (library bound) | ISBN 9781538338445 (6 pack)
Subjects: LCSH: Anxiety disorders--Juvenile literature. | Anxiety disorders--Treatment--Juvenile literature.
Classification: LCC RC531.D84 2019 | DDC 616.85'220651--dc23

Manufactured in the United States of America

CPSIA Compliance Information: Batch CSPK18: For further information, contact Rosen Publishing, New York, New York, at 1-800-237-9932.

CONTENTS

Words that look like **this** are explained in the glossary on page 31.

WHAT IS ANXIETY?

Anxiety is a word we use to describe the feelings of fear and worry that we all experience from time to time. For example, many of us feel anxious before performing on stage or taking a test. Our thoughts might race and we might feel like there are knots in our stomach. These feelings are completely normal. They can sometimes even be helpful because they let us know that what we are doing is important to us.

BEING ANXIOUS BEFORE A BIG SPORTS MATCH CAN HELP GIVE YOU THE ENERGY YOU NEED TO PERFORM AT YOUR BEST.

However, when feelings of worry stop us from doing things we like to do, or when they affect us all the time, even when nothing scary is happening, it is considered to be a mental health condition. A mental health condition is a condition that affects the brain, our thoughts, and our feelings. Both children and adults can have mental health conditions like anxiety. Often mental health conditions are diagnosed by a doctor or **therapist**.

FACT

WHEN ANXIETY AFFECTS OUR MENTAL HEALTH IT IS OFTEN CALLED GENERALIZED ANXIETY DISORDER.

WHAT DOES ANXIETY FEEL LIKE?

Anxiety is an emotion so it mainly affects your mood. It can feel like there are too many worrying ideas in your head at once. It can be distracting listening to all these different worries, making it difficult to concentrate on things like schoolwork or even fun things like playing games and reading books. It might feel very busy inside your head, like a computer that has too many programs running.

Although anxiety starts in your brain, it can affect the rest of your body in many ways. Think back to a time where you felt scared. You might have had a racing heart, shaky legs, or a stomachache. Maybe you felt very hot and short of breath. You might even have felt like crying or screaming. These are all **symptoms** of anxiety that happen in our bodies. They are nothing to worry about and will go away once you feel calm again.

ANXIETY AND THE BODY

These **physical** symptoms of anxiety can cause us to worry even more because they make us believe there is something wrong with us, or that we are ill. It is important to remember that, as uncomfortable and scary as these symptoms can be, they can't hurt you and they will go away when you feel calm again.

SOME OF THESE SYMPTOMS ARE:

BLURRED VISION

DIFFICULTY SWALLOWING

QUICK BREATHING

FEELING SICK

SWEATY HANDS

HEADACHE

SORE MUSCLES

RACING HEART OR **PALPITATIONS**

STOMACHACHE

JELLY LEGS

Dealing with anxiety is difficult, but it can be easier when you understand what is happening inside your brain. The emotions of worry and fear begin in the amygdala (a-MIG-du-luh), which are two almond-shaped parts of the brain that are responsible for warning you about danger. They are part of the limbic system, the system in the brain that deals with our emotions. The amygdala tells the hypothalamus – another part of the brain – to react to worry and **stress**.

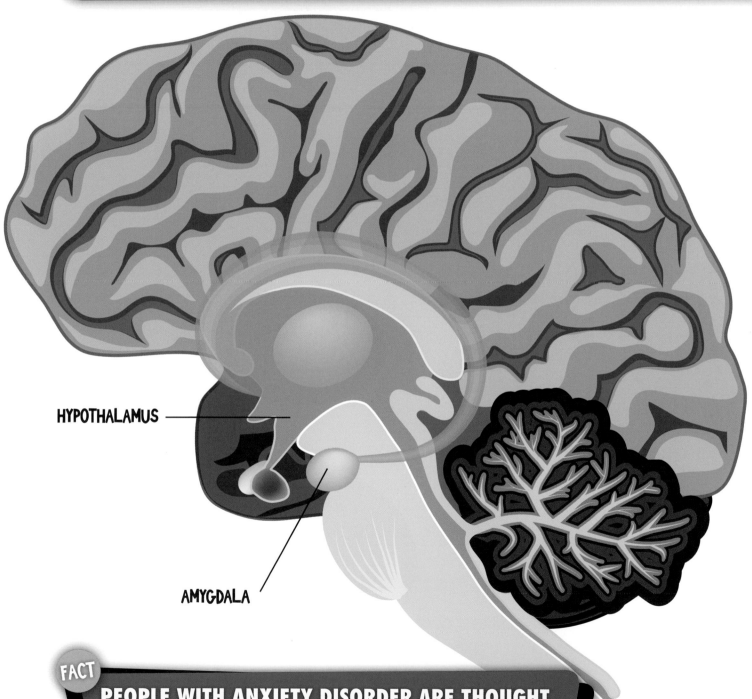

HYPOTHALAMUS

AMYGDALA

FACT

PEOPLE WITH ANXIETY DISORDER ARE THOUGHT TO HAVE AN OVERACTIVE AMYGDALA.

FIGHT OR FLIGHT

It is the job of your hypothalamus to begin something called the fight, flight, freeze response in your body. This is a full-body response that gives you the energy to either face your fears (fight) or run away from them (flight). The third response, freeze, can happen when we feel so overwhelmed that we feel like we can't move or are stuck.

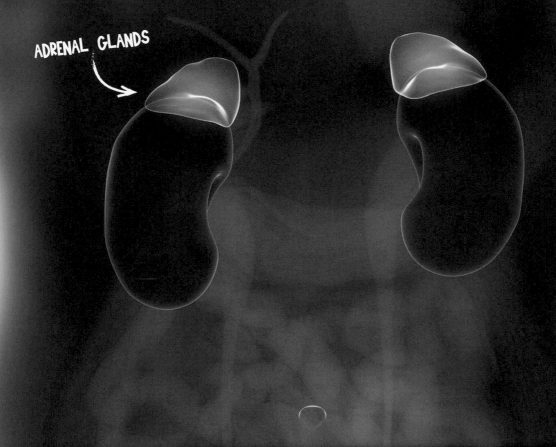

ADRENAL GLANDS

The hypothalamus tells two **glands** that sit above your kidneys, called your adrenal glands, to release a **hormone** called adrenaline (sometimes called epinephrine). These hormones tell certain parts of your body, such as your heart and lungs, to work harder so that you can fight or run away from the thing that is frightening you.

Scientists think humans have developed this response to fear because our **ancestors** needed to fight and run away from **predators**, like saber-toothed tigers. The freeze response may have even helped them to "play dead" by staying still long enough that a predator wouldn't notice them.

MANY SCIENTISTS BELIEVE THE REASON SOME HUMANS ARE SCARED OF THE DARK IS BECAUSE OUR ANCESTORS WERE MORE LIKELY TO BE ATTACKED BY PREDATORS IN THE DARK.

Today, however, the things that make us scared aren't always life-or-death situations and are often more complicated. For example, we might be scared of embarrassing ourselves in front of our friends, or we might be scared of failing a test. Humans are social animals, meaning that we work best when we live and work in large groups with many people. Being scared of doing things wrong in front of others would have helped our ancestors to stay part of the group or tribe.

This fight, flight, freeze response affects our body in many ways. It is the cause of the symptoms of anxiety listed on page 8. An adrenaline rush gives some parts of the body, such as the heart, lungs, and muscles, the energy they need to work harder. This is helpful if you need to run away from something. However, because it is such a powerful hormone, adrenaline can cause some unhelpful side effects when it floods the body. Exercise helps many people with anxiety to feel better. This is because it uses up the energy that an adrenaline rush causes.

FACT

NERVOUS HABITS SUCH AS NAIL BITING, TAPPING, OR JIGGLING YOUR LEG ARE ALSO WAYS THAT YOUR BODY TRIES TO GET RID OF EXTRA ENERGY.

If you don't need to run away from anything, fast-paced breathing can cause you to take in too much air. This is called hyperventilation (hi-per-vent-uh-LAY-shun) and can cause you to feel dizzy and faint. Your adrenal glands also release a hormone called cortisol. Cortisol can affect your digestive system. It makes your stomach produce acid to help break up your food. However, too much stomach acid when you don't need it can make you feel sick, or make you need to go to the bathroom more than usual.

PANIC ATTACKS

The fight, flight, freeze response is very important for keeping us safe from danger. For example, if you accidentally stepped into a road in front of a car, you would need a fast response in order to get out of the way quickly. However, for people with anxiety disorders, this response might happen when it is not needed, which can feel very frightening. This is called a panic attack.

If you are experiencing a panic attack you might:

- feel as if you are going to have a **heart attack**
- feel as if you are going to die
- feel as if you can't control your body
- feel like shouting or crying

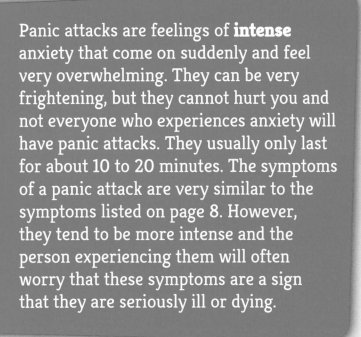

Panic attacks are feelings of **intense** anxiety that come on suddenly and feel very overwhelming. They can be very frightening, but they cannot hurt you and not everyone who experiences anxiety will have panic attacks. They usually only last for about 10 to 20 minutes. The symptoms of a panic attack are very similar to the symptoms listed on page 8. However, they tend to be more intense and the person experiencing them will often worry that these symptoms are a sign that they are seriously ill or dying.

FACT

PANIC ATTACKS MIGHT FEEL SCARY, BUT THEY ARE HARMLESS. YOU CAN'T GET ILL OR DIE FROM HAVING A PANIC ATTACK.

Panic attacks can happen when you are already anxious about something. For instance, if being in crowded places frightens you, then busy shopping malls might be a **trigger** for a panic attack. However, panic attacks can also happen without warning and people sometimes experience them when they are at home relaxing.

If you experience panic attacks, being aware of the things and situations that trigger your anxiety can help you to deal with them. It may even help to write down where you were and what you were doing when you had a panic attack. This can help you see which situations tend to act as triggers for your panic attacks. For example, if you were away on vacation every time you had a panic attack it could help you realize that sleeping away from home is a trigger for you.

For some people, the experience of having a panic attack leaves them scared that they will have another one. Because of this, they might avoid the situation they were in when they had the panic attack. For example, if someone had a panic attack during gym class at school, they might not want to join in gym activities anymore. It is important to remember that it isn't always the place you were in, or the activity you were doing, that caused the panic attack. Instead, panic attacks often happen because of a buildup of anxiety.

FACT

TO STOP PANIC ATTACKS FROM HAPPENING, IT'S ALWAYS HELPFUL TO TALK TO SOMEONE YOU TRUST ABOUT THE THINGS THAT ARE MAKING YOU ANXIOUS INSTEAD OF BOTTLING UP YOUR FEELINGS.

Some people feel embarrassed after having a panic attack in front of others. There is no reason to feel embarrassed for panicking, but it can help you to recover if there are fewer people around. Ask an adult if you can go somewhere quiet – don't just go off on your own.

CALMING DOWN

Sensory Grounding

You can think of panic attacks like fire drills. Sometimes fire alarms need to be tested to make sure they are still working. In the same way, the body needs to test our fight, flight, freeze responses. These tests tend to happen more often for people with anxiety. Luckily, there are many ways to calm down from a panic attack. Sensory grounding is just one of these ways. Sensory grounding is all about using your senses to become aware of your surroundings and feel more calm.

Sensory Grounding Method

1. START BY TAKING SLOW, DEEP BREATHS. BREATHE IN FOR THE COUNT OF FOUR AND OUT FOR SIX.

2. LOOK AROUND YOU. CAN YOU LIST FIVE THINGS THAT YOU CAN SEE? CAN YOU SEE PEOPLE AROUND YOU? WHAT COLOR IS THE FLOOR?

3. LISTEN UP. WHAT ARE FOUR THINGS YOU CAN HEAR? IT MIGHT BE PEOPLE TALKING, OR CARS DRIVING OUTSIDE.

4. PAY ATTENTION TO YOUR BODY. WHAT CAN YOU FEEL? PERHAPS YOU CAN FEEL YOUR CLOTHES ON YOUR SKIN. WHERE ARE YOU SITTING? CAN YOU FEEL THE FURNITURE UNDERNEATH YOU?

CASE STUDY: RANJIT

My name is Ranjit and I have anxiety. Sometimes it feels like I'm scared of everything. I get scared of answering questions in class in case I get them wrong and I get scared of school assemblies because they make me feel trapped. My biggest fear is being away from home. What if something awful happened to my mom and dad while I was at school? I want to have fun and concentrate on my work but these worries just won't leave me alone. It's even worse when we go on school trips. Everyone in my class loves them but I hate them. I can't stand being so far from home.

MY TEACHER USED TO CALL ME A WORRYWART. I DIDNT LIKE THIS NAME AS IT MADE MY WORRIES SEEM SILLY.

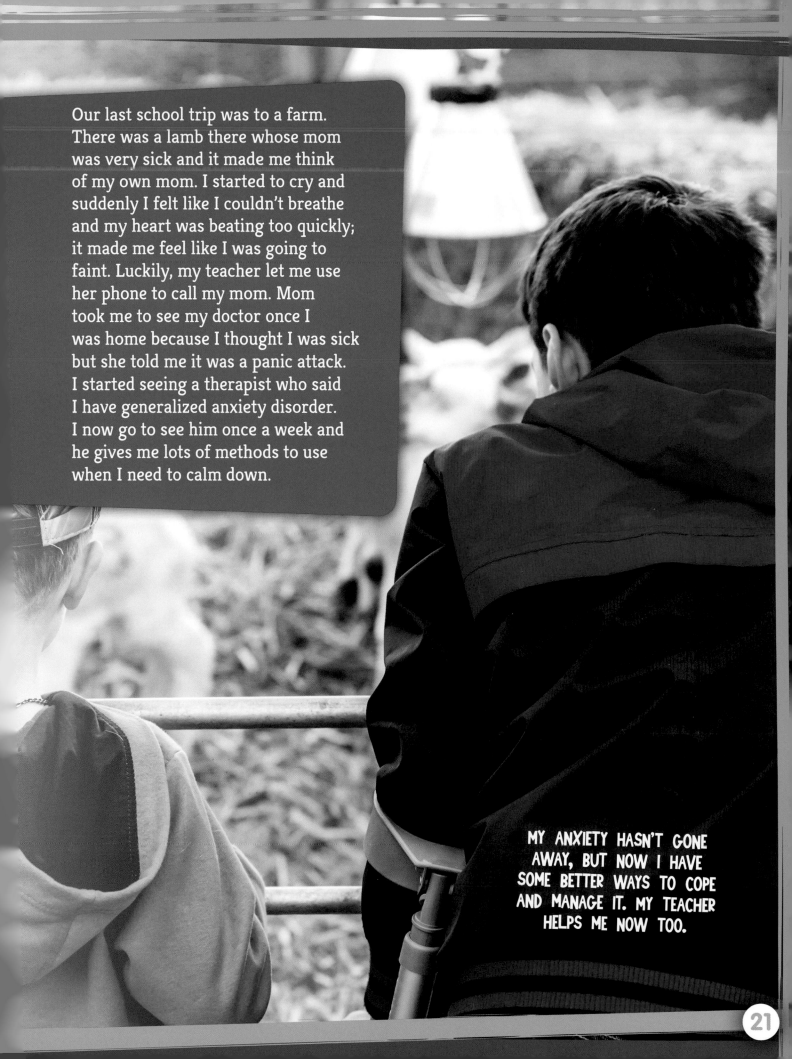

Our last school trip was to a farm. There was a lamb there whose mom was very sick and it made me think of my own mom. I started to cry and suddenly I felt like I couldn't breathe and my heart was beating too quickly; it made me feel like I was going to faint. Luckily, my teacher let me use her phone to call my mom. Mom took me to see my doctor once I was home because I thought I was sick but she told me it was a panic attack. I started seeing a therapist who said I have generalized anxiety disorder. I now go to see him once a week and he gives me lots of methods to use when I need to calm down.

MY ANXIETY HASN'T GONE AWAY, BUT NOW I HAVE SOME BETTER WAYS TO COPE AND MANAGE IT. MY TEACHER HELPS ME NOW TOO.

RELAXATION TECHNIQUES

Relaxation techniques are methods that anyone can use to calm down when they feel anxious. One of these techniques is called progressive muscle relaxation. This is where you relax the different muscles in your body, one at a time. Here's how to do it:

Step 1

Starting with your feet, squeeze the muscles in your toes as you inhale (breathe in) and relax them when you exhale (breathe out). Try to breathe in for a count of four and out for a count of six. If you relax your body, your mind will follow.

BUDDHISTS BELIEVE THAT TAKING TIME TO RELAX AND FOCUS ON YOUR BREATHING CAN HELP YOU CLEAR YOUR MIND OF WORRYING THOUGHTS. THIS IS CALLED MEDITATION.

Step 2

Using this method, work your way up your body, tensing and relaxing each different muscle as you go. After your toes, you can move on to your legs, hips, stomach, shoulders, arms and hands. Lastly, scrunch up your face as tight as you can for a count of four and then relax it. We hold a lot of tension in our jaws because we use them all the time for things like eating and talking. Relaxing your jaw can stop you from getting headaches.

DIFFERENT FEARS

There are two types of fears: rational fears and irrational fears. Rational fears are about things that are likely to happen and are in your control. For example, you might worry about forgetting your lines in an upcoming school play. It makes sense to worry about this at least a little bit as it will motivate you to practice your lines so you remember them on the night. Irrational fears are about things that are less likely to happen and are out of your control. For example, some people are scared of dogs. It makes sense to be scared of an angry, snarling dog; this could hurt you so your fear tells you to stay away and keeps you safe. But an irrational fear would be being afraid of a very friendly dog on a leash. That dog isn't scary – but if you are very frightened anyway, this is an irrational fear.

IRRATIONAL FEARS ARE OFTEN ABOUT THINGS THAT ARE UNLIKELY TO HURT YOU. BEING SCARED OF ONE THING IN PARTICULAR IS ALSO CALLED HAVING A PHOBIA.

LISTENING TO EACH OTHER CAN HELP US UNDERSTAND DIFFERENT KINDS OF FEARS.

Everybody has a mixture of both types of fears, but people with anxiety are more likely to have irrational fears or phobias. However, people with anxiety can also worry **excessively** about rational fears. Everybody has different fears and everyone's fears are important. No matter how someone's fear sounds to you, it is very real and frightening to them. We should always try to be understanding and treat everyone's rational and irrational fears equally.

CASE STUDY: KARINA

My name is Karina and I have lots of fears about lots of different things. When we learned about volcanoes at school, I got nightmares. When I saw on the news that a tornado had happened somewhere far away, I worried about that. Sometimes, I feel like I can't talk about my fears in case people think I'm being silly and overreacting. Once, we had a lesson all about the heart and how it pumps our blood around our body. Our teacher told us that it's important to be healthy so we don't get **heart disease** when we're older. This made me worry a lot. It sounded like a horrible thing to have.

One day I got very anxious in class and my heart started beating very fast. This made me worry even more. What if there was something wrong with it? I knew I wasn't allowed to leave the classroom without permission but I ran out anyway because I was so frightened. At first my teacher thought I was misbehaving, but after I told her why I left the room, she was very understanding. She told me that my fears aren't silly and that I can always talk to her about them. She also gave me a little blue card with the words "Time Out" on it. If I give it to her when I feel panicky, she will take me to the school nurse who can help me calm down.

PUTTING YOUR THOUGHTS INTO WORDS

Because we are not all scared of the same things, it can be hard for people to know you are feeling anxious unless you tell them. Physical illnesses, like chicken pox, have **visible** symptoms, like spots or a rash. Mental health conditions, like anxiety, often have no visible signs that suggest you are ill. Talking about our mental health is just as important as talking about our physical health. After all, the brain is a very important part of the body. Talking about how we are feeling can do amazing things for our mental health.

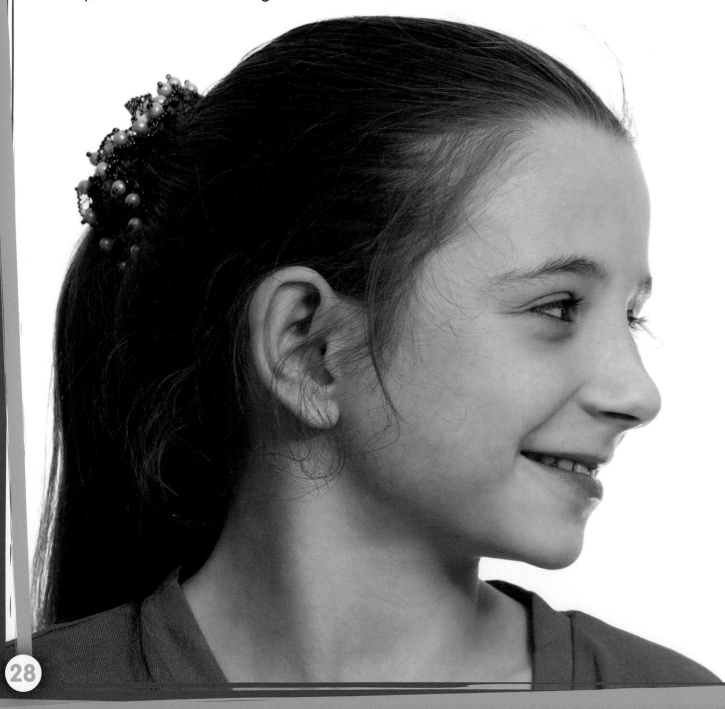

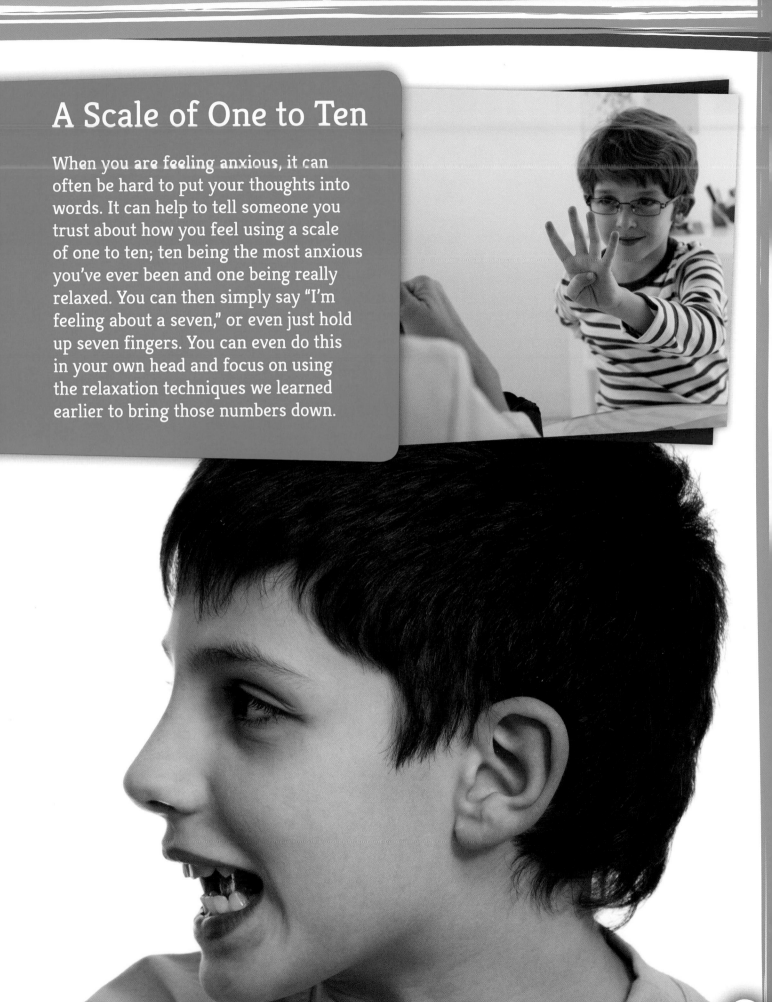

A Scale of One to Ten

When you are feeling anxious, it can often be hard to put your thoughts into words. It can help to tell someone you trust about how you feel using a scale of one to ten; ten being the most anxious you've ever been and one being really relaxed. You can then simply say "I'm feeling about a seven," or even just hold up seven fingers. You can even do this in your own head and focus on using the relaxation techniques we learned earlier to bring those numbers down.

TALKING TO SOMEONE

There are lots of people you can talk to about mental health problems like anxiety. You can talk to someone close to you, like a caregiver, family member or friend, or someone whose job it is to help you such as a teacher, doctor or counselor. Anxiety can make you feel like you are alone and that nobody else worries about the things you do, but that's not true. No matter how strange, embarrassing or complicated you think your worries are, it is always better to share them with someone else so they can help you feel better.

GLOSSARY

ancestors	persons from whom one is descended, for example a great-grandparent
Buddhists	people who follow the philosophy of Buddhism
excessively	to an amount that is more than what is wanted or needed
glands	organs in the body which produce chemical substances for the body to use or get rid of
heart attack	damage caused to the heart due to loss of blood supply
heart disease	any disease which affects the health of the heart
hormone	a chemical in your body that tells cells what to do
intense	to a strong degree
palpitations	noticeably rapid, strong, or irregular heartbeats
physical	relating to the body
predators	animals that hunt other animals for food
stress	a state of mental or emotional tension
symptoms	things that happen in the body suggesting that there is a disease or disorder
therapist	a person who is specially trained to treat mental health conditions
trigger	something that causes or sets off anxiety
visible	able to be seen

INDEX